# Simple
## Truths *of*
# Leadership

# Simple Truths of Leadership

### 52 Ways to Be a Servant Leader and Build Trust

## Ken Blanchard
## Randy Conley

SLII® is a registered trademark of The Ken Blanchard Companies®.
The One Minute Manager® is a registered trademark of The Ken Blanchard Companies®.

Berrett-Koehler Publishers, Inc.
1333 Broadway, Suite 1000
Oakland, CA 94612-1921
Tel: (510) 817-2277
Fax: (510) 817-2278
www.bkconnection.com

ORDERING INFORMATION
**Quantity sales.** Special discounts are available on quantity purchases by corporations, associations, and others. For details, contact the "Special Sales Department" at the Berrett-Koehler address above.
**Individual sales.** Berrett-Koehler publications are available through most bookstores. They can also be ordered directly from Berrett-Koehler: Tel: (800) 929-2929; Fax: (802) 864-7626; www.bkconnection.com.
**Orders for college textbook / course adoption use.** Please contact Berrett-Koehler: Tel: (800) 929-2929; Fax: (802) 864-7626.

Distributed to the U.S. trade and internationally by Penguin Random House Publisher Services.

Berrett-Koehler and the BK logo are registered trademarks of Berrett-Koehler Publishers, Inc.

Printed in Canada.
Berrett-Koehler books are printed on long-lasting acid-free paper. When it is available, we choose paper that has been manufactured by environmentally responsible processes. These may include using trees grown in sustainable forests, incorporating recycled paper, minimizing chlorine in bleaching, or recycling the energy produced at the paper mill.

Library of Congress Cataloging-in-Publication Data

Names: Blanchard, Kenneth H., author. | Conley, Randy, author.
Title: Simple truths of leadership : 52 ways to be a servant leader and
    build trust / Ken Blanchard, Randy Conley.
Description: 1 Edition. | Oakland, California : Berrett-Koehler, 2022. |
    Includes bibliographical references and index.
Identifiers: LCCN 2021034754 (print) | LCCN 2021034755 (ebook) | ISBN
    9781523000623 (hardcover) | ISBN 9781523000630 (adobe pdf) | ISBN
    9781523000647 (epub)
Subjects: LCSH: Leadership. | Trust.
Classification: LCC HD57.7 .B5633 2022 (print) | LCC HD57.7 (ebook) | DDC
    658.4/092—dc23
LC record available at https://lccn.loc.gov/2021034754
LC ebook record available at https://lccn.loc.gov/2021034755

First Edition
27  26  25  24  23  22  21      10  9  8  7  6  5  4  3  2  1
Book producer: PeopleSpeak
Text designer: Reider Books
Cover designer: Irene Morris

Ken dedicates this book to his family:

Margie, Scott, Madeleine, Debbie, and Tom McKee,

as well as the Leadership Team of

The Ken Blanchard Companies

for their amazing trusted servant leadership

that brought our company through a pandemic and back.

Good on them and everyone involved!

Randy dedicates this book to

Kim, Michael, and Matthew.

You inspire me every day

to be worthy of your trust.

# Contents

# Simple Truths

The beginning of my mission statement is "I am a loving teacher and an example of simple truths." That focus has been central in all of my work, including the study of servant leadership. I have always looked for simple truths that reflect commonsense practices people can use to make their work and life—as well as the lives of the people they care about—happier and more satisfying. To that end, I find it fun and inspiring to work with coauthors who share a similar philosophy—because I have always found that 1 + 1 is greater than 2.

That's certainly been the case as I have worked on this book with Randy Conley. Randy's focus over the last fifteen years has been on distilling the complex topic of trust into simple, actionable principles that help people experience more authentic and fulfilling relationships. In recognition of his work, Trust Across America awarded Randy a Lifetime Achievement Award for being a top thought leader in the field of trust. In addition, Inc.com named him a Top One Hundred Leadership Speaker and Thinker.

When it comes to servant leadership and trust, we both wonder why the principles we see as common sense are so seldom used in common practice. If today's leaders had a more commonsense approach to leadership, we'd venture to say that 65 to 70 percent of the workforce would not be considered disengaged.

That's one reason our original title for this book was *DUH! Why Isn't Commonsense Leadership Common Practice?* Another reason is that when I would mention that title to audiences, they'd roar with laughter as they recognized the truth in the title. I would immediately get questions about when the book was going to be available. However, when our publisher, Berrett-Koehler, sent out a survey about possible titles and subtitles, two things were clear: first, the word *duh* doesn't translate well from English to other languages; and second, a favorite title rose to the top—*Simple Truths of Leadership: 52 Ways to Be a Servant Leader and Build Trust*, with the cover tagline "Making Common Sense Common Practice."

We wrote this book because we know a lot of people aren't applying commonsense leadership principles in the workplace. The format for the book is simple. On the left page, we identify a Simple Truth about servant leadership or trust. On the right page, we describe the puzzling lack of use of the concept and briefly explain why it is important. The final element is a call to action for readers—"Making Common Sense Common Practice"—where we break down the concept into ideas that leaders can easily apply on the job. When commonsense leadership is put into practice, everybody wins—leaders, their people, and their organizations.

We've divided the Simple Truths we are sharing into two parts: "Servant Leadership," which features me, and "Building Trust," which features Randy. We have two reasons for doing this:

- When servant leadership is effectively implemented, trust abounds among leaders and their people. Servant leadership and trust go hand in hand.
- These two topics highlight our respective areas of expertise.

You can use this book in several ways. Read the Simple Truths in order, pick one truth to read and apply each week of the year, or jump to a subtopic that interests you most. At the end of the book, you'll find a discussion guide for exploring the concepts further with your team.

We hope you'll enjoy reading our book and making some of these Simple Truths an integral part of your leadership style. If you do, we know it will make a difference in your life and the lives of the people you influence.

—Ken

# PART ONE

# SERVANT
# LEADERSHIP

I n this part, Ken Blanchard takes the lead with a focus on his lifelong passion of servant leadership as an influence process in which leaders help their people accomplish goals.

Much of my work in the past was focused on leadership behavior and how to improve leadership style and methods. My colleagues and I attempted to change leaders from the outside. But in recent years, we have found that effective leadership is an inside job. It is a question of the heart. It's all about a leader's character and intention.

Why are you leading? Is it to serve or to be served? Answering this question truthfully is so important that I co-edited a book with Renee Broadwell entitled *Servant Leadership in Action: How You Can Achieve Great Relationships and Results*. In it, forty-five key leaders in our field, including Simon Sinek, Brené Brown, and Marshall Goldsmith, share their points of view about servant leadership. The essence of that book is *you can't fake being a servant leader.*

The most persistent barrier to being a servant leader is a heart motivated by self-interest that looks at the world as a "give a little, take a lot" proposition. Self-serving leaders put their own agenda, safety, status, and gratification ahead of others who are impacted by the leaders' thoughts and actions.

The shift from self-serving leadership to leadership that serves others is motivated by a change of heart. If leaders don't get their heart right, they will never become servant leaders. A misguided heart will color their thinking, impact their behavior, and cause them to begin every day by asking "What's in it for me today?" That's certainly not servant leadership.

In this part, you will learn more about servant leadership and the power it has to make the world a better place by focusing on the greater good.

—Ken

# The Essence of
# Servant Leadership

**SIMPLE TRUTH #1**

# Servant leadership is the best way to achieve both great results and great relationships.

Organizational leaders often have an either/or attitude toward results and people. For example, leaders who focus only on results may have trouble creating great relationships with their people and leaders who focus mainly on relationships may have trouble getting desired results.

Yet you can get both great results and great relationships if you understand the two parts of servant leadership:

- The *leadership* aspect focuses on vision, direction, and results—where you as a leader hope to take your people. Leaders should involve others in setting direction and determining desired results, but if people don't know where they're headed or what they're meant to accomplish, the fault lies with the leader.
- The *servant* aspect focuses on working side by side in relationship with your people. Once the vision and direction are clear, the leader's role shifts to service—helping people accomplish the agreed-upon goals.

### MAKING COMMON SENSE COMMON PRACTICE

This one-two punch of the aspects of servant leadership enables you to create both great results and great relationships:

1. Let your people know what they're being asked to do by setting the vision and direction with their help. In other words, vision and direction, while the responsibility of the leader, is not a top-down process.
2. During implementation, assure your people you are there to serve, not to be served. Your responsibility is to help them accomplish their goals through training, feedback, listening, and communication.

It's important for servant leaders to establish this both/and mindset toward results and relationships.

## SIMPLE TRUTH #2

# Evey great organization has a compelling vision.

W hen I explain what a compelling vision is to some leaders in organizations, they either give me a blank look or say something like "I'm sure we have one on the wall somewhere." So what is a compelling vision?

According to my book with Jesse Stoner, *Full Steam Ahead! Unleash the Power of Vision in Your Work and Your Life*, a compelling vision includes three elements: your purpose (what business you are in), your picture of the future (where you are going) and your values (what will guide your journey).

A compelling vision is alive and well in companies that are leaders in their field, such as Disney, Southwest Airlines, Nordstrom, Wegmans, and Starbucks.

### MAKING COMMON SENSE COMMON PRACTICE

Here's how you can incorporate the three elements of a compelling vision in your organization:

- Make sure the people in your organization know what business they are in. For example, when Walt Disney started his theme parks, he said, "We are in the happiness business."
- Confirm that your people know where they are going—what good results would look like. At Disney, the picture of the future is that all guests of the parks would have the same smile on their faces when leaving as when they entered.
- Find out if the people in your organization are clear on what values will guide their journey. Disney's first value is safety. Its next values are courtesy and "the show," which is about everyone playing their parts perfectly, whether they are a ticket taker or Mickey Mouse. Disney's final value is efficiency—having a well-run, profitable organization.

If you can share your compelling vision as clearly as Disney does, congratulations! You have just made common sense common practice.

**SIMPLE TRUTH #3**

Servant leaders turn
the traditional
pyramid upside down.

M ost organizations and leaders get into trouble during the implementation phase of servant leadership if the traditional hierarchical pyramid is used. When that happens, whom do people think they work for? The people above them. The minute you think you work for the person above you, you assume that person—your boss—is responsible and your job is to be responsive to your boss's whims or wishes. "Boss watching" can become a popular sport where people get promoted based on their upward-influencing skills. As a result, all the energy of the organization moves up the hierarchy, away from customers and the frontline folks who are closest to the action.

Servant leaders know how to correct this situation by philosophically turning the pyramid upside down when it comes to implementation. Now the customer contact people and the customers are at the top of the organization, and everyone in the leadership hierarchy works for them. This one change makes a major difference in who is responsible and who is responsive.

### MAKING COMMON SENSE COMMON PRACTICE

To make servant leadership come alive, implementation is key:

- Communicate to your people that you work for them, not the other way around. Your job is to serve, not to evaluate.
- Empower your people by letting them bring their brains to work. In this way, they become responsible—able to respond—to their internal and external customers. Your job is to be responsive to them, helping them accomplish their goals.

This creates a very different environment for implementation and makes it clear to everyone who is responsible and to whom.

# Secrets of the
# One Minute
# Manager

**SIMPLE TRUTH #4**

All good performance
starts with clear goals.

L eadership is about going somewhere. If you and your people don't know where you're going, your leadership doesn't matter. Although most managers agree with the importance of setting goals, many do not take the time to clearly develop goals with their team members and write them down. As a result, people tend to get caught in an activity trap where they are busy doing tasks—but not necessarily the right tasks.

To manage your team's performance, have one-on-one meetings with your people to establish observable and measurable goals around their key areas of responsibility. Then you and they will have clear performance indicators to help determine whether they are making progress or need coaching to improve.

### MAKING COMMON SENSE COMMON PRACTICE

To focus on what is important, set SMART goals with your people. "SMART" is a tried-and-true acronym for the most important factors in setting quality goals:

- *Specific*—A goal should be clear about what needs improvement and what good performance looks like.
- *Motivating*—People want to know that what they do makes a difference.
- *Attainable*—People like challenging goals that stretch them but are not impossible.
- *Relevant*—A goal should make a difference in overall performance.
- *Trackable*—A record-keeping system is necessary to regularly measure performance.

Effective performance management always begins with clear, observable, measurable goals.

## SIMPLE TRUTH #5

# The key to developing people is to catch them doing something right.

When I ask people in organizations around the world how they know whether they are doing a good job, the number one response is "Nobody has yelled at me lately. No news is good news." These people aren't being caught doing something right. They dread seeing their boss because they know the hammer is going to come down.

The most common leadership style I encounter is what I call *seagull management*, where managers set goals with people and then disappear until something goes wrong. Then they fly in, make a lot of noise, dump on everybody, and fly out.

That's why when people ask me what one concept I would want to hold on to if everything else I had taught over the last fifty years were taken away, I always cite the importance of catching people doing things right and praising them. An effective praising focuses on reinforcing behavior that moves people closer to their goals.

### MAKING COMMON SENSE COMMON PRACTICE

When you catch someone doing something right, follow these steps when you praise them:

1. Praise the person as soon as you notice them doing something right.
2. Let them know what they did right—be specific.
3. Tell them how good you feel about what they did right and how it helps.
4. Pause to give the person time to feel good about what they've done.
5. Encourage them to do more of the same.
6. Make it clear you have confidence in them and support their future success.

Praising is a powerful activity for both managers and team members. In fact, it is the key to training people and making winners of everyone you work with.

# SIMPLE TRUTH #6

# Praise progress!

Good performance is a moving target, not a final destination. Many well-intentioned leaders wait to praise their people until they do something exactly right, such as completing a project or accomplishing a goal. But unless the person is confident in the task area, the leader could be waiting forever. *Exactly* right behavior is made up of a series of *approximately* right behaviors. Praising someone's progress lets them know they're going in the right direction.

For example, suppose you want to teach a toddler to say, "Give me a glass of water, please." If you waited until she said the whole sentence before giving her a drink, she could die of thirst. Instead you start by saying, "Water! Water!" Suddenly one day, she says, "Waller." You jump around, hug and kiss her, and get Grandmother on the phone so the child can say, "Waller! Waller!" It isn't *water*, but it's close. You don't want a twenty-one-year-old going into a restaurant asking for a glass of waller, so after a while you accept only the word *water*. Then you start on *please*.

The same process works with adults. We all can use encouragement on the long road to victory.

### MAKING COMMON SENSE COMMON PRACTICE

It's easy to praise progress if you follow these four steps:

1. Get out of your office and wander around. For remote employees, have frequent video meetings to keep in touch.
2. Pay attention to what people are working on and how they are progressing.
3. When you catch someone doing something right—or in the beginning, approximately right—praise them.
4. Continue to cheer them on toward the desired behavior.

Servant leaders help their people achieve goals by coaching, encouraging, and praising them along the way.

## SIMPLE TRUTH #7

When people are off track, don't reprimand them—redirect them.

In *The One Minute Manager*, originally published in 1982, my coauthor, Spencer Johnson, and I called the Third Secret of the One Minute Manager "One Minute Reprimands." People used to see leadership as a top-down process. When someone was experienced with a task but performed poorly, their manager would give immediate feedback in the form of a quick "reprimand" of the behavior—not the individual—to help them get back on track.

Today, side-by-side leadership is proving far more effective. Because technology and other changes are happening so fast, people are almost always in a learning mode. Punishing a learner is never appropriate—so in *The New One Minute Manager*, Spencer and I changed the Third Secret to "One Minute Re-Directs."

When people are clear on the goal and still learning but their performance isn't up to standard, redirection is far more effective than a reprimand. The aim is to build people up so they will continue to move toward improved performance.

### MAKING COMMON SENSE COMMON PRACTICE

When a person who makes an error is still learning, follow these steps to give an effective redirection response:

1. Redirect the person as soon as possible.
2. As the leader, be sure you have made the goal clear. If not, clarify the goal.
3. Confirm the facts first and review the error together. Be specific about what went wrong.
4. Let them know how you feel about the error and its impact on results.
5. Pause for a moment to allow the person time to feel the effect of the error.
6. Tell them they are better than their mistake and you think well of them.
7. Remind them that you have trust in them and support their success.

# The best minute servant leaders spend is the one they invest in people.

People sometimes wonder why Spencer Johnson and I titled our book *The One Minute Manager*. They can't imagine how someone can manage in a minute. The reality is that many managers don't take the time, even a minute, to set goals for their people, praise their progress, or redirect their efforts—the Three Secrets from the book.

Investing a little .time in your people is similar. Part of *The One Minute Manager*'s significance is how it helps leaders understand that the best ways to serve your people don't have to involve long conversations, scheduled meetings, or performance reviews. Sometimes the simplest acts—like paying attention, commenting on what people are doing, or having a friendly chat—can be the most meaningful. Investing in people is about spending time focusing on them, not yourself.

### *MAKING COMMON SENSE COMMON PRACTICE*

The best minutes you invest in your people can focus on simple things:

- Listen to people's suggestions or discuss a problem.
- Ask people what they did over the weekend or how a sick family member is doing.
- Wish someone good luck on a presentation or say, "Happy Birthday."

Making people feel special doesn't have to take a lot of your time. Spending a few moments of your day to let them know you care could mean more to them than you'll ever know.

# A Situational
# Approach to
# Servant Leadership

**SIMPLE TRUTH #9**

Effective servant leaders
realize they have to
use different strokes
for different folks.

Through the years, I've observed that most managers have a favorite leadership style they always use with their people. In fact, our company's research shows 54 percent of managers use only one leadership style. They're one-trick ponies.

These managers have an either/or approach to leadership—they think they must focus on either results or people. Managers who restrict themselves to either extreme tend to be ineffective. But managers who are servant leaders flex their leadership style to each individual's development level for maximum performance. They know this both/and approach leads to both happier people and a more successful organization.

Any leadership style will work in some situations but not others. As we've proven with SLII®, our situational approach to effective leadership as described in the book *Leadership and the One Minute Manager*, managers need to use different strokes (leadership styles) for different folks, depending on their competence and commitment in their present job. For example, Enthusiastic Beginners (low competence, high commitment) need a Directive leadership style. Disillusioned Learners (some competence, low commitment) need a Coaching style. Capable, but Cautious, Contributors (high competence, variable commitment) need a Supportive leadership style. Finally, Self-Reliant Achievers (high competence, high commitment) need a Delegating style.

### *MAKING COMMON SENSE COMMON PRACTICE*

Make sure you have a flexible leadership style:

- Sit with each team member and look at their responsibilities.
- Determine whether they are generally an Enthusiastic Beginner; a Disillusioned Learner; a Capable, but Cautious, Contributor; or a Self-Reliant Achiever.

It won't take you long to realize you have to use different strokes for different folks.

## SIMPLE TRUTH #10

Effective servant leaders don't just use different strokes for *different* folks, they also use different strokes for the *same* folks.

It's interesting to observe managers who use the same leadership style with all their people all the time. They often are frustrated—as are their over- or undersupervised team members.

While individuals generally can be at a specific development level, which requires a certain leadership style, they might have one or two goals where their competence and commitment are different from their overall job knowledge. For example, a person who is generally considered to be a Self-Reliant Achiever can usually be delegated to and left on their own. However, if you give that person a new task where they have little experience, they might be considered an Enthusiastic Beginner on that task. If you delegate to them in this part of their job, it could backfire. Why? Given their development level on this particular task, they need a completely different leadership style—in this case, clear direction and close supervision.

Managers who are servant leaders take a situational approach to leading people. They know they sometimes need to use not only different strokes (leadership styles) for different folks but also different strokes for the *same* folks in different areas of their job.

### MAKING COMMON SENSE COMMON PRACTICE

Servant leaders who utilize the SLII® framework realize that leadership is not something you do *to* people, it's something you do *with* them:

- Lay out and agree on goals with your people.
- Teach them the SLII® model.
- Determine with each person what their development level is on each of their goals.

When you do this, you and your people will understand the benefit of using different leadership styles for different tasks or goals and you will be well on your way to being an effective servant leader.

# Create a Motivating Environment

**SIMPLE TRUTH #11**

Profit is the applause
you get for creating a
motivating environment
for your people so they
will take good care of
your customers.

S ome leaders worship the bottom line. They think the only reason to be in business is to make money. They don't understand that the best run and most profitable organizations know their number one customer is their people.

If you train, empower, and care about your people as your number one most important customer, they will go out of their way to take care of your organization's number two most important customer—the folks who buy your products and services. When that happens, those customers become raving fans of your organization and, in many ways, part of your sales force. This takes care of your company's bottom line and the financial interests of the owners or shareholders. Now that's a winning environment!

### MAKING COMMON SENSE COMMON PRACTICE

To create this winning environment as a servant leader, you must do two things:

1. Focus on your people by letting them know they are important to your organization and their contributions count, particularly in terms of satisfying customer needs.
2. Empower your frontline people to listen to their customers—both external and internal—act on their needs, and, in the process, exceed their expectations.

## SIMPLE TRUTH #12

# Create autonomy
# through boundaries.

W hen I talk to leaders about helping their people become autonomous, a lot of them think I mean they should give people the freedom to do anything they want. No—boundaries are necessary.

One of my favorite sayings is "A river without banks is a large puddle," taken from my book with John Carlos and Alan Randolph, *Empowerment Takes More Than a Minute.* You want people to have freedom within boundaries so they can accomplish their goals in a way that makes sense. Just as the banks of a river channel the power and energy of the water, so do effective boundaries channel the power and energy of your people.

### *MAKING COMMON SENSE COMMON PRACTICE*

Encourage people's autonomy within boundaries this way:

- Establish clear goals, expectations, and standards of performance.
- Ensure people are aware of all procedures, rules, and laws.
- Confirm everyone knows your organization's compelling vision:
  - Your purpose (what business you are in)
  - Your picture of the future (where you are going)
  - Your values (what will guide your journey)

**SIMPLE TRUTH #13**

# You get from people what you expect.

When people don't understand what their leaders expect of them, they feel lost. They have no compass, no boundaries, and no agreed-upon standards of conduct to follow. They're not sure how to please their boss, how to behave around their teammates, or what a good job looks like. All they can do is wait for someone to tell them what to do and how to do it.

As a servant leader who works side by side with your team members, you must let your people know exactly what you expect from them. This gives them a mental picture of how to be successful under your leadership.

But expectations aren't just about words—they are also about you modeling the behaviors you expect. You must walk your talk, or your words are meaningless. Communicating your expectations gives your people confidence and clarity about what a good job looks like.

## MAKING COMMON SENSE COMMON PRACTICE

For example, suppose you tell your people that your expectations of them are similar to the Golden Rule: Do unto others as you would have them do unto you. Describe to them in clear terms what that would look like:

- Act ethically in everything you do.
- Treat your customers the way you would want to be treated.
- Care for your teammates and cheer each other on.

Bravo! You've just painted a picture your people can see, feel, and apply to their daily work. These clear expectations, communicated directly to your team members, establish the standard for how you want them to consistently behave. Serve your people and help them accomplish their goals by setting the bar high and modeling the behavior you wish to see.

**SIMPLE TRUTH #14**

The best use of power
is in service to others.

**M**ost new leaders are excited to have power because they feel they finally have the title and position to do things their way. But having power doesn't guarantee cooperation from your people. Leaders who think they are a big deal because of their position are at risk of losing their best people and not getting the performance they need from the people who remain.

When I was elected president of the seventh grade, I came home from school excited to tell my parents about this achievement. My father, who retired as a rear admiral in the US Navy, had a quick reminder for me. "Congratulations, Ken. But now that you're president, don't use your position. Great leaders are great not because they have power but because their people trust and respect them."

My dad knew an important principle of being a successful servant leader: people will give you their best when they trust you and know you have their backs.

## *MAKING COMMON SENSE COMMON PRACTICE*

When you have a leadership position, focus not on the power that comes with the position but on the people you have an opportunity to serve. Your people will know you are there to serve, not to be served, when you do the following:

- Continually emphasize *we* over *me*.
- Listen more than you talk.
- Encourage and support people's efforts rather than directing them.

When your people are your focus, they know they are part of a team and are motivated to give you their best efforts.

**SIMPLE TRUTH #15**

Never assume you know
what motivates a person.

Most leaders think they know what motivates their people—either money or more responsibility. When you think that way, and one of your people is performing well, you might say one of two things:

- "I'm so pleased with your work; I've negotiated a nice raise for you." But in this case, the person doesn't have pressing financial needs and might be thinking, "What I'd really like instead is more responsibility around here."
- "In recognition of the great job you've been doing with customer relations, I'm giving you more responsibility." However, in this case the person has had health problems in the family and could use some extra cash.

You've now given a raise to someone who wants more responsibility and given more responsibility to someone who wants a raise. In both cases, you assumed you knew what motivated the person. The reality is that people have personal reasons for what motivates them.

### MAKING COMMON SENSE COMMON PRACTICE

Motivate your people in an effective and personal way:

- Ask them at the beginning of the year or the start of a new task what they would like as a reward if they do a good job.
- When they perform well, give them a proper praising and add, "Remember when I asked you what would motivate you to do a good job?" Then present them with their chosen reward.

# Characteristics of
# Servant Leaders

**SIMPLE TRUTH #16**

People with humility
don't think less of
themselves, they just
think of themselves less.

W hen I talk to people about humility as a key ingredient of servant leadership, they often see it as a weakness. And yet, when Norman Vincent Peale and I wrote *The Power of Ethical Management* in 1988, we used this Simple Truth to highlight the idea that people with a healthy self-esteem have a balance of pride sprinkled with a fair amount of humility.

Jim Collins, in his classic book *Good to Great*, determined that high performing leaders display a powerful mixture of personal humility and professional will. As Collins contends, "They're ambitious, to be sure, but ambitious first and foremost for the company, not themselves."

### MAKING COMMON SENSE COMMON PRACTICE

To bring humility into practice, Collins suggests that when things go well, ego-driven leaders look in the mirror and pat themselves on the back. When things go wrong, they look out the window to see who they can blame.

To be a servant leader, take these steps instead:

- When things go well, look out the window and give others the credit.
- When things go poorly, look in the mirror and take full responsibility—a hallmark of a servant leader.

How do you feel about humility now? Not a real weakness, is it? Neither is the fact that I am a raving fan of Jim Collins's work.

**SIMPLE TRUTH #17**

# It's okay to toot your own horn.

One reason some managers are hard on others is because they're also hard on themselves. They're always thinking, "I should've done that better" or "What a dummy I am, forgetting that detail." Unfortunately, sometimes poor self-expectations can influence other people's perceptions. It's not easy to be around people who are constantly putting themselves down or second-guessing themselves. It would be better if they occasionally caught themselves doing something right.

When you catch yourself doing things right, everything in your life will improve—especially your relationships. Why? Because it's fun to be around people who like themselves. And after all, if you're not your own best friend, who will be?

As my dad used to say, "If you don't toot your own horn, others might use it as a spittoon!"

### MAKING COMMON SENSE COMMON PRACTICE

If you find yourself always giving credit to others for their good efforts—although there's nothing wrong with that—remember that a little self-praise doesn't hurt.

- When people appreciate what you're doing, don't say, "Yes, but . . ." Instead, tell them you appreciate their noticing.
- Along the same lines, when someone pays you a compliment, simply smile and say, "Thank you." Don't disagree with them—that's like telling the person they don't have good judgment or aren't very smart.

If someone says or does something nice, accept it. Don't be afraid to pat yourself on the back once in a while. If you feel good about yourself, you'll find it easier to help others feel good about themselves too.

## SIMPLE TRUTH #18

# Don't work harder;
# work smarter.

While I think the amount of time and effort leaders put into their work is important, I know many leaders see a direct relationship between the amount of work they do and their success. They think the more time they put in, the more successful they'll look. *Delegation* is a foreign word. They have an internal critic that keeps saying "Don't just sit there, do something."

I guarantee those leaders are working late while their people are out having fun. In addition to doing their own job, they're working on tasks their people should be doing. They think delegating looks as if they are dodging their own responsibilities.

Servant leaders work smarter. They know their job isn't about doing their people's work for them. It's about preparing and training their people to do their own work, then getting out of their way so they can achieve their goals.

### MAKING COMMON SENSE COMMON PRACTICE

When someone brings you a problem—what Bill Oncken and I call a *monkey* in our book *The One Minute Manager Meets the Monkey*—don't say, "Let me think about it and I'll get back to you." If you do that, you might as well pull up a chair for the monkey. Instead, when someone brings you a monkey, take the following steps.

1. Pet the monkey and give advice on its care and feeding.
2. Make sure it goes out the door with its proper owner—your team member.

Working smarter not only means delegating, it also means helping people solve their own problems. If people bring you a problem and you own it, soon you are doing their job—and working harder, not smarter—while they are on the golf course or relaxing at home. Don't hesitate to delegate when it's appropriate. Nobody wants an office full of monkeys.

# SIMPLE TRUTH #19

"No one of us is as smart as all of us."

—Eunice Parisi-Carew
and Don Carew

I have met leaders in organizations around the world who act as if leadership is all about them. They want everybody to recognize that they are in charge.

People who think that way certainly aren't servant leaders. They are self-serving leaders who miss out on the reality that their people are capable of much more than they are given credit for. As a result, the best people exit the organization as soon as possible and search for a company where leaders see their people as partners rather than subordinates (subordinary people).

Servant leaders, on the other hand, realize leadership is about working alongside their people, sharing information, and keeping lines of communication open. When that happens, people get to know each other's strengths and build on them to help the team perform at the highest level. They prove that 1+1 is greater than 2.

## MAKING COMMON SENSE COMMON PRACTICE

If you want to create a high performing team, you need to do the following:

- Face the fact that your people already understand that you don't know everything.
- Ask for help from your team members when you are making decisions or trying to find solutions to problems.
- Let them know everyone's contribution is needed and appreciated.

When you model this side-by-side leadership philosophy, your team will be ready and willing to get on board.

**SIMPLE TRUTH #20**

Love is the answer.

What is the question?

# According to 1 Corinthians 13:4–7,

Love is patient, love is kind. It does not envy, it does
not boast, it is not proud.
It does not dishonor others, it is not self-seeking, it is
not easily angered,
it keeps no record of wrongs. Love does not delight in
evil but rejoices with the truth.
It always protects, always trusts, always hopes, always
perseveres.

Most people have heard this passage on love read at weddings or other special occasions. I don't know a better representation of the qualities of a servant leader than the virtues listed in this passage.

But if you ask someone who works for a self-serving leader to describe their boss, you'll hear the opposite of these characteristics. Self-serving leaders are seldom perceived as patient or kind. They tend to envy others with more influence, brag about their accomplishments, and so on.

I believe servant leadership is love in action. And if love is the answer, perhaps the question is, What do servant leaders lead with?

## MAKING COMMON SENSE COMMON PRACTICE

Want to know if your people see you as a servant leader?

1. List the personal traits from this passage and ask people which ones describe you as a leader. Make it anonymous.
2. Once you get the feedback, set up a meeting with your team, share what you've learned, and ask them how you could improve on the traits where you scored low.
3. Then—this is key—make changes in your leadership style to show them you are serious about improving.

# What Servant
# Leaders Need
# to Know

Servant leaders don't
command people to
obey; they invite
people to follow.

I've met a number of leaders who get upset when they give an order and people don't obey it immediately. They think when you are a leader, if you tell people what to do, they should blindly submit.

The reality is that most people don't like to be told to do something. They like to be involved in decisions. That's why I talk about servant leadership being a better way of leading than top-down, command-and-control leadership. Servant leaders know people want to be part of the team. They invite their people to follow them in a side-by-side working relationship that the people have had a part in creating.

## MAKING COMMON SENSE COMMON PRACTICE

If you want people to follow your leadership invitation, take the following steps:

- Focus on *we* more than *me*.
- Continually let team members know why they are important and how they can contribute to the success of the team.
- Use your language wisely as it makes a difference when talking to team members. "Would you mind?" comes across as an invitation. "Do this for me" sounds more like a command.
- Say the words *please* and *thank you;* they are always welcome in any relationship.

Leading by command and position doesn't work. To make a difference in the world, you need to gather a cohesive team of people who want to follow your lead.

## SIMPLE TRUTH #22

People who plan the
battle rarely battle
the plan.

In most organizations, leaders get behind closed doors, hatch a change initiative to fix a problem they think exists, and then roll out the plan to their teams. But people have a hard time getting behind an organizational change effort they have had no part in creating. Too many leaders think all the brains are in the executive wing and they don't need the input of others.

Great leaders understand they are only as good as the people they gather around them. They know involving people early in a change initiative is critical to its success. People have predictable concerns about organizational change. When they can play a part in implementing the plan and are allowed to express their concerns and contribute their ideas and feedback, they are more likely to align behind the plan and help accomplish it.

## MAKING COMMON SENSE COMMON PRACTICE

Here's how to address people's primary concerns about change and how to get them involved, taken from the book *Leading at a Higher Level*:

- *Information concerns*—People want to know what you know. Share information about the change to prevent rumors and confusion. Keep communicating verified facts.
- *Personal concerns*—People want to know how the change will affect them. Let them express their feelings, and be ready with answers to their questions.
- *Implementation concerns*—People want to know how to perform in the face of change. Involve them in finding ways forward. You need their buy-in to succeed.
- *Impact concerns*—People want to know whether the change is working. Be encouraging, focus on the positive impact of people's efforts, and recognize their successes.
- *Refinement concerns*—People want to keep improving systems and processes. Continue to practice these leadership strategies, and keep lines of communication open.

## SIMPLE TRUTH #23

# Servant leaders
# love feedback.

Have you ever given feedback to someone up the hierarchy who killed the messenger? Maybe you made an honest comment like, "Boss, I think our Thursday afternoon meetings are a waste of time." Your boss shouted, "What do you mean 'a waste of time'? Are you kidding? Those meetings are important!" It's clear this self-serving leader doesn't want to hear the truth. Self-serving leaders hate feedback because, to them, negative feedback means you don't think they should lead anymore. That's their worst nightmare because they believe they *are* their position.

Servant leaders love feedback. The only reason they're leading is to serve—and if someone has suggestions on how they can serve better, they want to hear them. They don't allow their ego to get in the way. They look at feedback as a gift.

Giving and receiving feedback without judgment is one of the best strategies for servant leaders who strive to achieve both great relationships and great results.

### *MAKING COMMON SENSE COMMON PRACTICE*

If you truly want to know what your team members think of your leadership style, discuss it with them:

- Assure your people you won't get defensive when they give you feedback. Giving feedback to the boss doesn't come naturally to most people, so getting honest feedback from your team members may be difficult. They may fear being the messenger bearing bad news, so they hesitate to be candid. But if you open the door for them, you may learn many valuable nuggets of truth.
- Remember, they're giving you a gift, so make sure the first thing you say is "Thank you!" Then follow up with "This is so helpful. Is there anything else you think I should know?"

I think my colleague Rick Tate said it best when he said, "Feedback is the breakfast of champions!"

## SIMPLE TRUTH #24

People who produce good results feel good about themselves.

W hen people read the statement "People who produce good results feel good about themselves," most say, "Really? Shouldn't it be 'People who feel good about themselves produce good results'?" Sure, that's important—but in talking to and observing people, I have found what really motivates them and makes them feel good about themselves is producing good results. Why? Because results are tangible and observable—not only by people themselves but also by their peers.

For example, money usually motivates people only if it is feedback on results. Have you ever received a raise you were pleased with only to find out that somebody else who you didn't think worked as hard as you got the same—or even better—raise? Not only was that increase in pay not motivating, it became demotivating once you knew it had nothing to do with results. Suddenly, it didn't matter how hard you had worked.

### MAKING COMMON SENSE COMMON PRACTICE

It's hard for people to feel good about themselves if they are constantly falling short of their goals. That's why it's so important for you as a servant leader to do everything you can to help your people win—accomplish their goals—by ensuring the following:

- Make sure your people's goals are clear, observable, and measurable.
- As their leader, work together with your people to track progress.
- When performance is going well or falling short of expectations, give them appropriate praising, redirecting, or coaching—or reexamine whether your leadership style matches the person's development level on a specific goal.

People who feel good about the work they do are always looking for ways to contribute to the success of your organization.

W hen good work is done by teams, the leaders often like to pat themselves on the back and take all the credit. (Could there be an ego issue here?) I immediately became a raving fan of Rick Warren's book *The Purpose Driven Life* when I read his first line: "It's not about you." The goal of effective servant leaders is to serve their people and make sure they know their contributions are valued. These leaders realize that leadership is not about them—it's about the people they serve.

## *MAKING COMMON SENSE COMMON PRACTICE*

Model behaviors that show your people your goal is to serve, not to be served.

- When your team performs well and kudos come your way, make sure to step back and let most of the credit flow to your people.
- Continue celebrating team wins, whether it's with gift cards for everyone, a festive meeting where individual achievements are called out, or another form of praise or reward.

When people are recognized for their efforts, they will continue to be excited about their work. Eventually, they won't need as much external recognition—even from you—because they will begin to catch themselves doing things right.

The ultimate result of training people to be the masters of their own fate is reflected in this quote from the ancient Chinese philosopher Lao-tzu: "When the best leader's work is done, their people say, 'We did it ourselves.'"

# SIMPLE TRUTH #26

# Great leaders SERVE.

Self-serving leaders love top-down leadership. The last thing on their minds is working alongside their people as a servant leader. They're too busy commanding and controlling.

A central philosophy in the book *The Secret: What Great Leaders Know and Do* is "Great Leaders SERVE." My coauthor, Mark Miller, and I use the acronym SERVE to explain five essential ways great leaders serve.

## MAKING COMMON SENSE COMMON PRACTICE

If you are a leader who wants to serve, not to be served, follow these steps from the SERVE model:

- *See the future*—It's impossible to overstate the importance of a compelling vision. Once that clear vision is established, goals and strategies can be developed within the context of the vision.
- *Engage and develop people*—After the vision and direction are set, servant leaders focus on engaging and developing people so that they can achieve their goals and live according to the vision.
- *Reinvent continuously*—Servant leaders are lifelong learners who demonstrate a desire for continuous improvement. They see the organizational structure as fluid and are ready to adapt it to best serve the company, its customers, and its people.
- *Value results and relationships*—Both results and relationships are critical for long-term business survival. Treat your people well, they'll treat your customers well, and results will follow.
- *Embody the values*—Servant leadership is built on trust. Servant leaders must be living examples of their values to earn and sustain their people's trust.

The SERVE acronym is how servant leaders operate. Being successful in all five of these areas isn't easy, but it's well worth the effort—because servant leadership is love in action.

# PART TWO

# BUILDING
# TRUST

R andy Conley takes the lead in this part, focusing on
his expertise on the topic of trust as the foundation of
a successful organization. Leadership based on trust
is crucial for collaboration, innovation, employee commitment, and a healthy work environment.

Let me ask you a question: do you believe trust is important
to your success as a leader? If so, raise your hand. Okay, you
can put your hand down now.

Why do I think you raised your hand? Because nearly
everyone who hears that question raises their hand. Anyone would be hard-pressed to argue that trust isn't critically
important to leadership success.

Now let me ask you a second question: do you have a
defined strategy and plan for building trust? If so, raise your
hand. Anyone?

If you didn't raise your hand, don't feel bad; you're not alone. Most people don't raise their hand when I ask them that question. Why is that? Trust is like oxygen—most people don't think about it until they don't have any.

It can be difficult to know where to start. Trust goes deep and wide. There aren't any magic solutions when it comes to building trust. It requires a comprehensive and sustained approach over time.

That's where servant leadership comes in. Servant leadership is the vehicle to building trust. Servant leaders act in ways that inspire trust in their followers. In his seminal 1970 essay "The Servant as Leader," Robert K. Greenleaf, the father of the modern-day servant leadership movement, wrote that becoming a servant leader "begins with the natural feeling that one wants to serve, to serve first. Then conscious choice brings one to aspire to lead."

Servant leaders are distinguished by putting the needs of their followers ahead of their own. When team members believe their leader has their best interests at heart and is there to support them in achieving their goals, trust in their leader grows by leaps and bounds.

Trust is an outcome, a result of the behaviors we use in our interactions with others. If we act in trustworthy ways, we build trust. If we behave in an untrustworthy manner, we erode trust. It's common sense—but not always common practice.

That brings me to these Simple Truths about building trust. They contain nuggets of wisdom on topics such as the role of trust in leadership, the importance of honesty and integrity and treating people fairly, characteristics of trustworthy leaders, ways to build trust during change and rebuild broken trust, and the incredible power of forgiveness.

It's my hope these Simple Truths will inspire and equip you to be the leader your people deserve. Because everyone should have a leader they can trust.

—Randy

# Trust in Leadership

**SIMPLE TRUTH #27**

Leadership begins
with trust.

Some leaders charge headlong into setting strategies and goals for their teams without giving much thought to building trust. Yet trust is the foundation of any successful, healthy relationship. When you have the trust of your team, all things are possible. Creativity, innovation, productivity, efficiency, and morale flourish. If your team doesn't trust you, you get resistance, disengagement, apathy, and, ultimately, failure.

The most successful leaders realize their number one priority is to build trust with their team. Trustworthy leaders demonstrate competence in their roles, act with integrity, show care and concern for team members, and honor their commitments by following through on their promises.

### MAKING COMMON SENSE COMMON PRACTICE

Does your team perceive you as trustworthy? If you're not sure, ask them. Here are a few sample questions:

- Do you have confidence in my leadership/management abilities? Where or how can I improve?
- Do I walk my talk? Where can I be more consistent in my behavior?
- How well do I listen to you? Do our interactions leave you feeling heard, valued, and supported?
- Am I dependable? Do you trust that I'll follow through on my commitments?

Demonstrating your vulnerability by having a discussion with your people about trust is a powerful way to introduce servant leadership in your workplace.

**SIMPLE TRUTH #28**

Building trust is a skill
that can be learned
and developed.

I n my work, I have found that people have a common misconception about trust. Many people believe trust just happens, through some sort of relationship osmosis. The truth is that building trust is a skill. And, as with any skill, we can learn it and become better at it with practice. Since trust is either built or eroded by the behaviors we choose to use, we can enjoy more trust in our relationships when we use the right kind of behaviors.

## MAKING COMMON SENSE COMMON PRACTICE

In the book *Trust Works!* Ken and his coauthors Cynthia Olmstead and Martha Lawrence share the ABCDs of building trust. I have built on this work by coauthoring our company's Building Trust training program that teaches leaders how to build trust.

Follow these four aspects of the ABCD model to create trust:

- *Able*—Demonstrate competence.
- *Believable*—Act with integrity.
- *Connected*—Show care and concern for others.
- *Dependable*—Honor commitments.

Practicing these ABCD behaviors will foster a growing culture of trust in your relationships at every level, both at home and at work.

## SIMPLE TRUTH #29

## "Self-trust is the first secret of success."

—Ralph Waldo Emerson

What does it mean to trust yourself? It means to have a confident belief in your mission as a leader. I've known leaders who have never taken the time to clearly identify their leadership point of view. What motivates you as a leader? What are your values? What are your beliefs about leading others? If you don't know the answers to these questions, your leadership could be drawn off course.

A leader without a clear purpose is like a ship without a rudder—it is taken wherever the wind blows. But when you have a clear mission statement like Ken's ("I am a loving teacher and an example of simple truths"), your energy is channeled in a specific direction. Self-trust begins when you are clear on your leadership mission.

### MAKING COMMON SENSE COMMON PRACTICE

Writing your leadership point of view can help you become more authentic, self-aware, and intentional. You can develop your leadership point of view through the following steps, taken from the book *Leading at a Higher Level*. This may sound like a simple exercise, but it can lead to profound discovery about yourself and your leadership style:

1. List the key events and people in your life that have shaped your beliefs about leadership.
2. What lessons have you learned from these key events and people?
3. Based on those lessons, what are your top three to five values when leading others?
4. As a result, what can your team expect from your leadership in the future?
5. What are your expectations of yourself and of others going forward?
6. What is the leadership legacy that you want to leave?

Take your time to think through your answers to these important questions. When you are finished writing, share your work with your team.

## SIMPLE TRUTH #30

Someone must make the first move to extend trust. Leaders go first.

Y ou don't need trust if there's nothing at risk. That's called certainty, a sure thing, a guarantee. But if there is risk—if there is a chance you might get burned extending your love, money, or faith to someone else—then trust is essential. A part of that risk involves someone making the first move in extending trust.

Trust doesn't happen by accident. For trust to develop in a relationship, one party has to make the decision to extend trust in the hope it will be reciprocated. That's the way it works. Ernest Hemingway summed this up, simply yet eloquently, when he said, "The way to make people trust-worthy is to trust them."

In the workplace, it's your job as a leader to extend trust to your people first. It's not their job to have blind faith in you simply by virtue of your power or position of authority.

### *MAKING COMMON SENSE COMMON PRACTICE*

Think of a risky situation you are facing where you may be hesitant to trust someone. What would it look like for you to extend trust to that person?

- Don't trust blindly—that's foolish.
- Assess the other person's trustworthiness by examining how their behavior reflects the ABCDs of trust (see Simple Truth #28), then extend trust appropriately.

You won't know whether you can trust someone until you make the first move. My bet is they will prove themselves trustworthy and rise to the occasion.

## SIMPLE TRUTH #31

"People admire your strengths, but they respect your honesty regarding your vulnerability."

—Colleen Barrett

Too many leaders are closed books when it comes to relating to their teams. They are distant and detached, both physically and emotionally. Like the Wizard of Oz, many leaders are afraid to have team members look "behind the curtain" for fear they will be seen as less than perfect. This fear keeps team members from really getting to know the person behind the title or position.

Colleen Barrett, president emerita of Southwest Airlines and Ken's coauthor on the book *Lead with LUV*, has a great take on vulnerability in leadership: "I think when you're vulnerable, people realize that you, too, are human. And, perhaps even more importantly, they love your ownership of your personal positive and negative characteristics."

When people observe their leader exhibiting vulnerability, it can motivate them to do the same.

### *MAKING COMMON SENSE COMMON PRACTICE*

Consider taking these practical steps to be more vulnerable with your people:

- Focus on others, not yourself. Being self-oriented drives you to act in ways that preserve your carefully curated public image. Instead, focus on serving others and meeting their needs.
- Lead with humility. Humble leaders put themselves on the same level as their team members and are willing to be real with others. No pretenses, no masks—just you.

# Trust in
# Relationships

**SIMPLE TRUTH #32**

# There's no trust
# without *us*.

The world's current polarized political and social climate often pits people against each other with little room in the middle. This either/or mentality is shaping the way we build trust in relationships.

We must remember that in its purest form, trust is a psychological and emotional construct between two people. There's no trust without *us*—you and me, two people willing to take a risk and be vulnerable in front of each other with the expectation that the other won't take advantage. We don't demand it of each other, but we give it willingly because the other person has demonstrated their trustworthiness over time. And we constantly nurture the trust in these relationships so they continue to grow over time and work in a reciprocal fashion to constantly strengthen themselves. That's the *us* in trust.

### *MAKING COMMON SENSE COMMON PRACTICE*

Abraham Lincoln purportedly said, "I don't like that man. I must get to know him better." Identify someone in your life you are at odds with or have low trust in. How can you get to know them better and build a higher level of trust with them? Consider asking them these questions:

- What brings you joy?
- What really makes you angry?
- Who is your hero?
- What motivates you to work hard?
- What is your favorite thing about your job/career?
- What is your favorite book and why?
- If you could choose to do anything for a day, what would it be?

## SIMPLE TRUTH #33

# Fear is the enemy of trust.

I've observed many leaders manage people through fear and intimidation. They think pointing out mistakes, being critical, or even yelling at team members will get them to perform better. However, the long-term result is more likely to be people who either tune out the leader or fail to take initiative because they are afraid to make mistakes.

Even if you aren't the stereotypical loud, in-your-face type of boss, you may be casting a shadow of fear over your team without realizing it. Your positional authority alone is enough to create a certain amount of anxiety in the hearts of your employees. Mix in other fear-inducing behaviors like hoarding information or losing your temper, and you've got a recipe for creating timid—even fearful—team members.

Fear is the enemy of trust. It's virtually impossible for trust to survive if there is fear in a relationship.

### MAKING COMMON SENSE COMMON PRACTICE

You can gain trust and lower—or, ideally, eliminate—the amount of fear in your relationships with those whom you lead by taking these steps:

- Be consistent in your behavior. If your employees can reasonably predict how you'll react in a given situation, they won't be afraid to take risks.
- Treat mistakes as learning opportunities. High-trust cultures give employees confidence to set BHAGs—big, hairy, audacious goals—and risk failure by not achieving them. Rather than penalize your employees when they make a mistake, use the opportunity to coach them on how to do better the next time around.
- Be nice. Say "please," "thank you," and "you're welcome" when warranted. A little kindness goes a long way in building trust. Making the effort to be friendly and encouraging signals to people that you care about them.

## SIMPLE TRUTH #34

A relationship with no
trust is like a cell phone
with no service or
internet— all you can
do is play games.

Too many leaders treat relationships like a game. They view their team members as pawns on the chessboard of corporate politics that need to be maneuvered to accomplish the leader's goals.

Authenticity is an essential component of being a trustworthy leader. People long to follow a leader who is sincere—and when they find one, they will offer that leader 100 percent of their energy and engagement. An authentic person is genuine. They don't put on pretenses. "What you see is what you get" describes them. Their behavior in any given situation can be reasonably predictable, which breeds high levels of trust and security.

### MAKING COMMON SENSE COMMON PRACTICE

It's not hard to be authentic; all you have to do is be yourself. Authentic leaders display humility, admit what they don't know, walk their talk, own up to their mistakes, and do what they say they will do. You can be more authentic by being REAL:

- Reveal information about yourself. Let your team get to know you as a person, not just a boss.
- Engage people as individuals. Everyone wants to be seen as an individual, not just a number who shows up to do a job.
- Acknowledge team member contributions. People are starving for praise and recognition for their good work. Give it to them!
- Listen to learn. When you interact with people, spend more time listening than talking. Look for ways to incorporate their feedback and ideas into your decisions.

**SIMPLE TRUTH #35**

People don't care how
much you know until
they know how
much you care.

The higher some leaders move in an organization, the more they think they need to be the smartest person in the room. They believe showing off their brilliance will earn the trust and admiration of their people.

It doesn't matter how intelligent or charismatic you are as a leader—if your people don't think you have their best interests in mind and truly care for them, they won't give you their trust, loyalty, and best efforts. Demonstrating care and concern for others is the quickest and easiest way to build trust.

## MAKING COMMON SENSE COMMON PRACTICE

To gain trust with your people, start by building rapport. Building rapport isn't rocket science, but it does take intentional effort. Here are a few easy and practical ways to get started:

- Remember people's names and use them often.
- Strike up a conversation about them—not about you.
- Learn something about team members' lives outside of work.
- Share information about yourself when it comes up naturally.
- Look for mutual interests.

## SIMPLE TRUTH #36

"People will forget what you said, people will forget what you did, but people will never forget how you made them feel."

—Maya Angelou

Leadership is a matter of the heart. As a leader, it's important for you to say and do all the right things— but if people don't believe you truly care about them, you won't earn their trust. The way you make people feel is the true measure of your impact on them.

Are you treating your team members with respect, care, and consideration? Remember, you are the topic of conversation at the dinner table of every person who reports to you. What do they say about you?

## *MAKING COMMON SENSE COMMON PRACTICE*

Play show-and-tell with your team on a regular basis—but not the same show-and-tell game you remember from elementary school:

- Show your team you care through friendly camaraderie and acts of kindness. Demonstrate your care through your actions.
- Tell your team members how much you appreciate and value their work by catching them doing things right and praising them. People never tire of being told they're doing a good job.

As a servant leader, when you establish a sincere, caring environment through your words and actions, you can be assured your people will always remember you for the way you made them feel.

# Characteristics of
# Trusted Leaders

## SIMPLE TRUTH #37

"Your actions speak so loudly I cannot hear what you are saying."

—Anonymous

Our experience has shown that many leaders are good at making announcements but often fall short of following through on their bold proclamations. Talking about what you're going to do is easy; actually doing it is what builds trust with others. Henry Ford once said, "You can't build a reputation on what you are going to do." He knew what all trustworthy leaders know: your actions speak much louder than your words.

Walking your talk is the essence of integrity. The word integrity is derived from the Latin *integritas* or *integer*. It suggests the heart of the matter—whole, complete, not fragmented. When your behavior aligns with your speech, you are complete, whole, and acting with integrity.

What would your people say about your integrity? Are you a "do as I say, not as I do" kind of leader? If so, you're eroding trust with your people.

### MAKING COMMON SENSE COMMON PRACTICE

Assess yourself across the five *P*s of ethical leaders that Ken and Norman Vincent Peale describe in their book *The Power of Ethical Management*. Where are you strong and where do you need to improve?

- *Purpose*—Be driven by your purpose and use it to guide your actions.
- *Pride*—Show a sense of healthy pride. Unlike false pride, which stems from a distorted sense of self-importance, healthy pride springs from a positive self-image and confidence in one's abilities.
- *Patience*—Have faith that things will work out well as long as you adhere to your values and principles.
- *Persistence*—Stay the course and remain true to your purpose and values.
- *Perspective*—Keep the big picture in mind and understand what's truly important.

## SIMPLE TRUTH #38

# Tell the truth.
# Always.
# It's that simple.

Leaders who rationalize the truth often find themselves in quicksand. They look for ways to shape the truth in an effort to convince themselves they are being honest without telling the full story. But telling half truths is telling half lies.

Leaders erode trust when they spin the truth rather than being transparent in their communication. Spinning the truth is manipulation, which is perhaps a bit more socially acceptable than outright lying, but it's manipulation nonetheless.

Save spin for the gym, not the workplace.

### *MAKING COMMON SENSE COMMON PRACTICE*

Here's how you can avoid spinning the truth and, instead, build trust with your people:

- Think of situations when you've been tempted to be less than honest. Perhaps it was when you made a mistake but were embarrassed to admit it. Or maybe your team goofed up and you didn't want to look bad as a leader.
- Look out for examples that involve your ego and pride, which are often at the root of dishonest behavior. Do whatever it takes to prevent ego and pride from destroying your integrity.

The heart of trustworthiness is integrity—and you can't have integrity unless you are honest. Servant leaders always tell the truth. It really is that simple.

**SIMPLE TRUTH #39**

Don't ever make a
promise you can't keep.

The word *promise* has lost some of its reverence in today's culture. Leaders casually use the word as an expression of intent to follow through on a commitment—but they don't always have a solid plan in place to live up to their promises.

A broken promise is a major trustbuster. Few things erode people's trust more than a leader who makes empty promises. Why is that? Think back to when you were a child and one of your parents made a promise and didn't follow through. Remember the disappointment you felt?

A promise creates an expectation. When that expectation isn't met, trust is broken. Be careful when you use the word *promise*. Only say it if you have a surefire plan to make something happen!

### MAKING COMMON SENSE COMMON PRACTICE

Follow these tips to help you make reasonable promises you can keep:

- Make sure you have the resources (time, money, tools, people, etc.) needed to fulfill your commitment.
- Pinpoint how the promise connects to your core values so you'll have the sustained motivation to follow through.
- Identify the risks to your relationships should you fail to deliver on your commitment.
- Write the promise on your to-do list or calendar so you don't forget it.

## SIMPLE TRUTH #40

"There's nothing so unequal as the equal treatment of unequals."

—Anonymous

When I talk to people about building trust in the workplace, the topic of fairness inevitably comes to the forefront. For example, I make the statement "I'm being fair because I'm treating everyone _____." When I ask people to then fill in the blank, most answer, "the same."

The truth is, one of the most unfair things a leader can do is give everyone the same broad-brush treatment. Most leaders default to treating everyone the same because it's expedient. It's the path of least resistance—the leader doesn't have to worry about being accused of playing favorites. In reality, it's a leadership cop-out.

High-trust leaders understand the need to treat people equitably and ethically, given each person's situation. Leadership isn't always a one-size-fits-all. Of course, certain rules, policies, and legalities require everyone to be treated the same—but when it comes to the matter of leading individuals, you need to treat each person situationally.

### MAKING COMMON SENSE COMMON PRACTICE

How can you be fair and build trust with team members? Here are a few suggestions:

- Be transparent. Share information liberally and frequently.
- Increase involvement in decision-making. People who are involved in forming a decision have more ownership in implementing it.
- Play by the rules. Hold yourself and others accountable.
- Don't play favorites. No one likes a teacher's pet—so don't create one.

**SIMPLE TRUTH #41**

# #Trust is always trending. Doing the right thing never goes out of style.

A s a pioneer in the modern leadership development movement, Ken has seen many leadership trends and fads come and go over the years. One constant that never goes out of style is trust.

Great leaders understand they build trust through the consistency of their actions. They focus on doing the right thing even when it's uncomfortable or unpopular. That's because they know there is never a right time to do the wrong thing. When you're tempted to jump on the latest trending #leadershipfad, consider staying consistent with the one thing that's always trending: trust.

## MAKING COMMON SENSE COMMON PRACTICE

Our values drive our decisions. Servant leaders build trust because they are clear on the values that motivate their actions and guide their journey. Spend time doing an inventory of your personal values and choose the ones you hold most dear:

1. Write a long list of qualities that have meaning to you (for example, fairness, wisdom, generosity, courage, creativity, honesty, trustworthiness, etc.)
2. Narrow down the values on that list to the ten most important ones in your life.
3. When you're finished, choose your top three to five from that list.
4. Rank in order those top three to five values, beginning with the one most important to you.
5. Finish the following sentence for each value: "I am living according to this value whenever I . . ." In other words, define each value for yourself.

This isn't an exercise to rush through. It takes some soul searching and quiet, thoughtful time. But when you are finished, you will understand yourself, your motivations, and your intentions better than you did before. This clarity will lead to self-trust and help you build trusting relationships with people around you.

**SIMPLE TRUTH #42**

True servant leaders
admit their mistakes.

A common fallacy is that leaders should know all the answers. Because too many leaders believe this is true, they are afraid to admit their mistakes. They think owning up to a mistake means admitting failure, which makes them look weak in front of their team. In reality, admitting mistakes is one of the most powerful ways a leader can build trust. When your team sees you own up to your behavior, they see a leader who is genuine, honest, and authentic. They see a leader who is able to set aside their ego for the betterment of the team.

If you make a mistake, own it. Admit what you did, apologize if necessary, and then put a plan in place to not repeat the mistake. You'll find this will turbocharge the level of trust you have with your team.

### *MAKING COMMON SENSE COMMON PRACTICE*

When you admit a mistake, it is an excellent learning opportunity for your team. It gives you a chance to model servant leadership in action. Here are some best practices you can follow:

- Be prompt. Address the mistake as soon as possible. Delay can make it appear you're trying to avoid or cover up the issue.
- Accept responsibility. Own your behavior and any damage it caused.
- Highlight the learning. Let your team know what you've learned and what you'll do differently next time.
- Be brief. Don't overapologize or beat yourself up. Mistakes happen.

## SIMPLE TRUTH #43

Since we were given two
ears and one mouth,
we should listen more
than we speak.

When I ask people to describe the key character-istics of a great leader, being a good listener is always one of the first mentioned. People love to feel that their thoughts not only are heard but might even make a difference.

What's the difference between a good listener and a poor one? Good listeners focus on the other person and what they are saying. If someone says, "It's a beautiful day!" a good lis-tener's response is apt to be something like, "It sure is! What do you like best about it?" On the other hand, bad listeners focus on themselves. Their response to the comment about it being a beautiful day will likely take the discussion in a self-oriented direction, such as, "You call this beautiful? You should've seen where I was last week."

Poor listeners relate everything to themselves. Good lis-teners make you feel good because they're interested in you and what you are thinking and feeling. If your team mem-bers believe you are a great listener, they will share their best thinking with you.

### MAKING COMMON SENSE COMMON PRACTICE

Practice these skills to improve your ability to listen:

- Don't interrupt. It's rude and disrespectful to the speaker and conveys the attitude that what you have to say is more important than what they're talking about.
- Make sure you understand. Occasionally paraphrase or restate what you heard the person say to confirm you're tracking correctly.
- Listen for what's *not* being said. Ask open-ended ques-tions to explore what's truly at the heart of the matter.
- Stay in the moment. Resist the urge to let your mind drift. Take notes, listen actively, and stay engaged in the conversation.

# Trust and Control

## SIMPLE TRUTH #44

The most important part of leadership is what happens when you're not there.

High-control leaders are reluctant to delegate to their team members. They're concerned that when they're not around, people will get off course and do something stupid that will reflect badly on the leader.

Servant leaders develop and empower their people so that they will perform just as well, if not better, on their own as they do when the leader is present.

The classic example of this is the virtual workplace. When you as the leader are physically located alongside your people, it's easy to observe their working behaviors. But in today's world where so many people work remotely, that's an impossibility. The real proof that you are a trusted servant leader is how your people perform on their own. They know you trust them and they want to live up to the standards you have demonstrated.

### MAKING COMMON SENSE COMMON PRACTICE

Trusting your folks to do the work doesn't mean you are blindly placing trust in them; you're making a decision based on their competence and commitment to their tasks or goals.

Here are some ways to empower your people:

- Provide your team members the direction and support they need to accomplish their goals.
- Let them know you're there if they need help.
- Now step aside and watch them shine!

## SIMPLE TRUTH #45

# The opposite of trust is not distrust—it's control.

Many leaders like to play their cards close to the vest. They are afraid to give up too much control for fear that something will come back to bite them. They think it isn't worth the risk to give up control.

Because giving up control opens the door to risk, it makes these leaders more vulnerable to being hurt. In response, they withhold trust and try to control people and situations around them to protect their own safety. The result of this behavior is a culture of uncertainty.

If we define control as that which we have direct and complete power over, we quickly realize we don't possess that much control. We may be able to influence people or situations, but we can't control them. The only control we truly have is over ourselves: our actions, attitudes, values, emotions, and opinions.

People often assume mistrust or distrust is the opposite of trust, but that's not true. Control is the opposite of trust. Are you willing to give up control and trust others?

## *MAKING COMMON SENSE COMMON PRACTICE*

If you struggle to relinquish control and trust others, start with baby steps:

1. Identify low-risk situations where you feel comfortable extending trust.
2. Assess a person's trustworthiness by gauging their competence to handle the task, integrity to do the right thing, and commitment to follow through.
3. As you become more comfortable giving up control and learn that others can be trusted, extend more trust as situations allow.

## SIMPLE TRUTH #46

People don't resist change; they resist being controlled.

One of the great myths about change is that people automatically resist it. The truth is, most people don't actually resist the change itself. They resist being told to change and forced to go along with it. In reality, they resist being controlled.

While it is not always practical to involve people in planning a change strategy, it is important that they know the reasons the change is needed and the anticipated advantages of effectively implementing it. The more leaders involve their team members in the change process—by soliciting their ideas and opinions and sharing information—the less controlled people feel and the more open they will be to the change effort.

### *MAKING COMMON SENSE COMMON PRACTICE*

Part of a leader's job is to initiate change. Organizations are living organisms, and all living beings grow and change. The challenge for leaders is to help people not only accept change but also embrace the opportunities it presents. Here are some tips to consider:

- Even if your team members don't have a vote in the change, give them a voice.
- Proactively ask them for their ideas about the change and solicit their concerns.
- Pay special attention to addressing their concerns about how the change will personally affect them.
- Involve them in identifying what is under their control and how they can best adapt to the change.

**SIMPLE TRUTH #47**

People without accurate
information cannot act
responsibly, but people
with accurate information
are compelled to
act responsibly.

Simple Truth #47 is from the book *Empowerment Takes More Than a Minute,* coauthored by Ken, John Carlos, and Alan Randolph. I love this quote because it illustrates the importance of trust.

Leaders who don't trust others don't share information. They keep everything under lock and key. In the absence of information, people often make up their own version of the truth, which may be more negative than reality. When people don't have accurate information, it's as if their leader is handcuffing them from being their best.

Servant leaders trust their people and realize that openly sharing information about themselves and the organization is the right thing to do. When people have accurate information, they can make decisions that are in the best interests of the organization.

### *MAKING COMMON SENSE COMMON PRACTICE*

Great leaders understand that trust is the foundation of effective leadership. A key aspect of trust is sharing information with your people. Here are some tips on how to do it:

- Create a culture of accountability by providing access to information. If you aren't at liberty to share certain details, say so. Your people will understand.
- Speak plainly in ways that are easily understood. Present complicated data in simple terms and focus on having a dialogue with people, not bombarding them with trivia.
- Be a straight shooter. Your team members are adults who can handle the truth. Use healthy doses of compassion and empathy when delivering tough news.

# Restoring
# Broken Trust

**SIMPLE TRUTH #48**

Building trust is
a journey, not a
destination.

When I work with leaders on building trust, I often hear, "I don't need to learn how to build trust. People already trust me." These leaders see trust as a destination—something to achieve—and once you have it, you don't need to actively work at keeping it.

The truth is that building and keeping trust is a journey, an ongoing process of demonstrating trustworthiness. Like any journey in life, there will be days where the travel is smooth and easy and times when the road is rough and bumpy. We will inevitably do something to erode trust—and when that happens, it's good to have a process to follow to rebuild it. Trust can usually be restored if both parties are willing to work at it.

### MAKING COMMON SENSE COMMON PRACTICE

If you have eroded trust in a relationship, follow this process to begin restoring it:

1. Acknowledge. The first step in restoring trust is to acknowledge there is a problem. Identify the cause of low trust and what behaviors you need to change.
2. Apologize. Take ownership of your role in eroding trust and express remorse for the harm it has caused.
3. Act. Commit to not repeating the behavior and act in a more trustworthy way in the future.

Depending on the circumstances, it may take some time to fully restore trust in a relationship—but it can be done. Remember, building trust is a lifelong journey. There is no final destination.

For more on how to restore trust, read Ken's book with Margret McBride, *The 4th Secret of the One Minute Manager*.

**SIMPLE TRUTH #49**

A successful apology
is essential in
rebuilding trust.

When a relationship becomes fractured and an apology is warranted, many people assume the "guilty" person should be the one to apologize. The truth is, most times there is plenty of blame to be shared by both parties. Delivering a successful apology is essential to rebuilding trust that's been eroded.

One thing Ken and I have learned over the years is how to apologize. As of this writing, we have experienced more than ninety-two years of combined marriage with our spouses—fifty-nine for Ken and Margie, thirty-three for Kim and me. We've messed up a lot, so we've had plenty of practice apologizing, and we've found a good apology goes a long way toward restoring trust.

## MAKING COMMON SENSE COMMON PRACTICE

Think about a relationship of yours that has been damaged because an apology has never been given—whether by you or the other person. Follow the advice below to give an apology and get the relationship back on the right track.

- If you messed up, admit it. An effective apology includes an acceptance of responsibility.
- Don't use conditional language like *if* or *but* in your apology—that makes it sound as if you're trying to shift blame or make excuses.
- Pick the right time to apologize. Make sure the other person is ready and willing to hear you out.
- Be sincere and express remorse for your actions when you apologize.
- Acknowledge the pain you caused and let the other person share their feelings. It's important to listen without judgment or rebuttal.
- Commit to not repeating the behavior. An apology is only as effective as your attempt to not repeat the actions that eroded trust in the first place.

**SIMPLE TRUTH #50**

Apologizing is
not necessarily an
admission of guilt,
but it is an admission
of responsibility.

"I'm not going to apologize because I didn't do anything wrong!"

I remember my kids uttering this phrase a number of times when they were young. I've also heard it from leaders in the workplace more times than I care to remember. No one likes to be wrongly accused, and most people certainly don't want to apologize for something they didn't do. The thought of apologizing when you've done nothing wrong can make you feel indignant or defensive, which only makes the situation worse.

However, there is a time and place for apologizing when you're not guilty. It's important to remember that apologizing is not an admission of guilt; it's an admission of responsibility. You are taking responsibility for improving the relationship and moving past the situation at hand.

### *MAKING COMMON SENSE COMMON PRACTICE*

Here are three good reasons to apologize even when you've done nothing wrong:

- Choose the relationship over being right. Instead of playing the blame game or gloating in self-righteousness, muster up the emotional maturity to prioritize the relationship over your ego.
- Play the long game. All relationships have conflict. Use wisdom to discern when it's better to apologize, even if you're in the right, for the sake of preserving the long-term health of the relationship.
- Take one for the team. You may not have been at fault personally, but if your team has dropped the ball, you should take the blame on their behalf. Servant leaders give their team the credit when they succeed and take personal accountability when they fail. That's the responsibility of leadership.

**SIMPLE TRUTH #51**

Choosing not to forgive someone is like taking poison and waiting for the other person to die.

L eaders need to have tough skin and soft hearts. Inevitably, leaders will experience someone breaking their trust. Those occasions are choice points for leaders. They can harbor resentment and let it poison themselves and the relationship, or they can choose to forgive and work to mend the relationship.

When you choose not to forgive someone, it hurts only yourself. It fosters negative thinking, puts you on guard with others, and limits your ability to lead with authenticity. Do yourself a favor and choose forgiveness. You'll feel a weight lifted from your shoulders.

## *MAKING COMMON SENSE COMMON PRACTICE*

If you've been wronged in some manner and are struggling to forgive the other person, here are some tips:

- Choose your response. Your response shapes your reputation. Do you want to be known as a person who leads at a higher level or one who holds grudges?
- Lose the battle to win the war. Wise leaders have learned to pick their battles. In most cases it's smarter to forgive someone (lose the battle) to preserve the relationship (win the war).
- Remember that forgiveness doesn't eliminate consequences. Some people are reticent to forgive because they think it lets the other person off the hook for what they did wrong. Not true. People will experience consequences for their behavior.
- Forgive but don't necessarily forget. Nothing can erase the past, but forgiveness is about looking to the future. Forgiveness allows you to move forward in healing and hope.

**SIMPLE TRUTH #52**

# Forgiveness is letting go of all hope for a better past.

When someone breaks our trust, it can be hard to forgive—especially if it was a major betrayal. It's easy to believe that by refusing to forgive, we somehow hold power over the person who disappointed us. We think our refusal to grant forgiveness will make us feel better because we're withholding something the other person values and needs to move on—our forgiveness.

But whether or not you choose to forgive won't change what happened. You can't revise history to make it better. Choosing forgiveness allows you to reconcile the past with the present. It allows you to let go and move into the future unencumbered from the pain of past disappointments.

### *MAKING COMMON SENSE COMMON PRACTICE*

People have two common misconceptions that hold them back from extending forgiveness to others. Don't let these prevent you from making this commonsense principle common practice.

- Myth: Forgiving makes you a weakling or a doormat. Wrong. Allowing repeated violations of your trust is never a good idea, but forgiving others while adhering to healthy boundaries is a sign of strength.
- Myth: Forgiveness is dependent on the other person showing remorse. Not true. Whether or not the person who violated your trust apologizes or shows remorse for their behavior, the decision to forgive rests solely with you. Forgiveness can't be earned by the offender; it can only be given by the offended.

# Making Common Sense Common Practice in Your Leadership and Life

We are certain a number of these Simple Truths have been meaningful to you. We think that's wonderful, and we're grateful for the opportunity to share them with you.

But that's not enough! Now it's time to turn common sense into common practice. We want to remind you *why* it's important to be a trusted servant leader and *how* you can get there.

## *WHY BECOME A SERVANT LEADER, TRUSTED BY YOUR PEOPLE?*

The world is in desperate need of a new kind of leadership. The type of leadership we've seen in past decades has produced record low levels of trust and engagement in the workforce. Clearly, what we've been doing isn't working. We need a leadership philosophy grounded in the knowledge and belief that the most successful leaders and organizations are those that place an emphasis on serving others and leading with trust.

Trusted servant leaders are the answer to today's challenges. People are looking for deeper purpose and meaning as a way to meet the rapid changes happening in their lives. They are also looking for leaders they can trust and believe in—leaders whose focus is on serving the greater good.

Servant leadership is not just another management technique. It is a way of life for those with servant hearts. In organizations run by trusted servant leaders, serving others becomes the norm. The byproducts are better leadership, better service, a higher performing organization, and more success and significance.

## HOW CAN YOU GET THERE?

An ancient Chinese proverb says, "A journey of a thousand miles begins with a single step." We've made it easy for you to take that first step.

It's no coincidence we've shared fifty-two Simple Truths—one for each week of the year. Each week, choose a Simple Truth and focus on turning its commonsense wisdom into common practice. You can work through them sequentially from one to fifty-two, randomly pick one each week, or alternate between the "Servant Leadership" and "Building Trust" parts—whatever works best for you.

We've also included a discussion guide to help you reflect on these truths more deeply. This guide contains prompts from each of the servant leadership and trust subtopics we've addressed. You can use it for personal reflection, or you can explore the prompts with a colleague or your team. Once again, do whatever works best for you.

We believe leadership is more than a job. It's a calling. We all have a tremendous opportunity—and responsibility—to positively influence everyone we lead. When you've finished reading this book, resist the urge to say to yourself, "Oh, that was nice," and put it on your bookshelf to collect dust. Instead, keep it on your desk, refer to it often, and share it with a friend.

We are confident that after reading this book and putting these commonsense truths into common practice, you will be better equipped to lead at a higher level as a trusted servant leader.

Now, go and do it!

—Ken and Randy

# *Simple Truths of Leadership*
# Discussion Guide

We hope reading *Simple Truths of Leadership* has been an enjoyable experience that has given you a few new insights into what it means to be a servant leader and to build trust.

Perhaps you're interested in taking a deeper dive into the subject areas we've covered.

Here are twenty-four discussion prompts that touch on topics relating to servant leadership and trust. There are no right or wrong answers, no scores to add up or rankings to judge how well you do.

We invite you to present these prompts in a group of two or more individuals interested in sharing ideas, feelings, and beliefs about leadership and trust. Or, if you're more inclined toward independent study, please allow these prompts to provoke your thinking and bring you closer to the trusted servant leader you strive to be.

—Ken and Randy

## THE ESSENCE OF SERVANT LEADERSHIP

1. Do you think turning the hierarchical pyramid upside down would make it easier to be a leader or more difficult? Why?
2. Can you describe your company's compelling vision— its purpose, picture of the future, and values—as you understand it?

## SECRETS OF THE ONE MINUTE MANAGER

3. How can catching someone doing something right or redirecting them move them closer to their goals?
4. Share a true story that involved praising progress. What was the result?

## A SITUATIONAL APPROACH TO SERVANT LEADERSHIP

5. Share your favorite leadership style or styles. Describe one or two situations where that style may not be effective.
6. Think about a time when you had a boss who used a completely different leadership style from the one you needed. What happened?

## CREATE A MOTIVATING ENVIRONMENT

7. Share some specific ways to get your customers to become "part of your sales force."
8. What might happen if you made your expectations clear to your people but did not model your behavior on the same expectations? Why would that be a problem?

## CHARACTERISTICS OF SERVANT LEADERS

9. Do you think servant leaders can be humble and have a healthy self-esteem at the same time? How would that play out in the workplace?

10. How vulnerable would you feel having your team members describe you as a leader using the characteristics from the passage on love in Simple Truth #20? Do you think you would be able to make the changes necessary to improve yourself in their eyes?

## WHAT SERVANT LEADERS NEED TO KNOW

11. How would you feel about asking for feedback from your people in an organized and caring way? Would it help or hurt your leadership to know firsthand what your people think about you?

12. Which comes first: (a) people who produce good results feel good about themselves or (b) people who feel good about themselves produce good results? Why?

## TRUST IN LEADERSHIP

13. Are you confident enough in your people's trust to ask them the questions listed in Simple Truth #27? What do you think their answers will be?

14. Why might it be difficult to be the first one to extend trust? Have you known someone who trusted you before you had earned their trust? How did that make you feel?

## TRUST IN RELATIONSHIPS

15. When you read the Lincoln quote "I don't like that man. I must get to know him better," what feelings did that evoke in you? Picture yourself having those feelings.

What would you do to get to know someone you didn't like?

16. Can you tell if a leader is being authentic with you? How? Do you think your people see you as authentic? Why or why not?

## CHARACTERISTICS OF TRUSTED LEADERS

17. "One of the most unfair things a leader can do is give everyone the same broad-brush treatment." What does this statement mean to you? What's wrong with treating all people the same?

18. How can admitting a mistake be a good way to build trust with your people?

## TRUST AND CONTROL

19. If your team members are scattered all around the country (maybe the world), how can you trust they are working as hard as they would be if you were sitting near them in the same building?

20. Why is it important for leaders to share information with their people? Why do you think it's difficult for some leaders to do this?

## RESTORING BROKEN TRUST

21. How do you feel about the concept that servant leaders should take the blame if their team fails on a project or initiative? Is being accountable for their people's mistakes the responsibility of a servant leader?

22. Do you tend to forgive easily, or do you hold grudges? Explain why you are more likely to do one than the other.

## TWO FINAL QUESTIONS

23. Which of the fifty-two Simple Truths do you perceive to be a strength that you want to continue to leverage as a trusted servant leader?

24. Which of the fifty-two Simple Truths do you see as an opportunity for personal growth that you'd like to develop in your journey toward being a trusted servant leader?

# Works Cited

Blanchard, Ken, and Colleen Barrett. *Lead with LUV: A Different Way to Create Real Success*. Upper Saddle River, NJ: FT Press, 2011. (Simple Truth #31)

Blanchard, Ken, and Renee Broadwell. *Servant Leadership in Action: How You Can Achieve Great Relationships and Results*. Oakland: Berrett-Koehler, 2018. (Pages 5–6)

Blanchard, Ken, John P. Carlos, and Alan Randolph. *Empowerment Takes More Than a Minute*. San Francisco: Berrett-Koehler, 1996. (Simple Truths #12 and #47)

Blanchard, Ken, et al. *Leading at a Higher Level: Blanchard on Leadership and Creating High Performing Organizations*. Upper Saddle River, NJ: FT Press, 2019. (Simple Truths #22 [chapter 14 with Pat Zigarmi and Judd Hoekstra] and #29 [chapter 19 with Margie Blanchard and Pat Zigarmi])

Blanchard, Ken, and Spencer Johnson. *The One Minute Manager*. New York: HarperCollins, 2003, and *The New One Minute Manager*. New York: HarperCollins, 2015. (Simple Truths #7 and #8)

Blanchard, Ken, and Margret McBride. *The 4th Secret of the One Minute Manager: A Powerful Way to Make Things Better*. New

York: William Morrow, 2008; previously published as *The One Minute Apology*. New York: William Morrow, 2003. (Simple Truth #48).

Blanchard, Ken, and Mark Miller. *The Secret: What Great Leaders Know and Do*. San Francisco: Berrett-Koehler, 2004. (Simple Truth #26)

Blanchard, Ken, Cynthia Olmstead, and Martha Lawrence. *Trust Works! Four Keys to Building Lasting Relationships*. New York: William Morrow, 2013. (Simple Truth #28)

Blanchard, Ken, William Oncken Jr., and Hal Burrows. *The One Minute Manager Meets the Monkey*. New York: William Morrow, 1989. (Simple Truth #18)

Blanchard, Ken, and Norman Vincent Peale. *The Power of Ethical Management*. New York: William Morrow, 1988. (Simple Truths #16 and #37)

Blanchard, Ken, and Jesse Lyn Stoner. *Full Steam Ahead! Unleash the Power of Vision in Your Work and Your Life*. San Francisco: Berrett-Koehler, 2011. (Simple Truth #2)

Blanchard, Ken, Patricia Zigarmi, and Drea Zigarmi. *Leadership and the One Minute Manager*. New York: Harper Collins, 2013. (Simple Truths #9 and #10)

Collins, Jim. *Good to Great: Why Some Companies Make the Leap . . . and Others Don't*. New York: HarperCollins, 2001. (Simple Truth #16)

Warren, Rick. *The Purpose Driven Life: What on Earth Am I Here For?* Grand Rapids, MI: Zondervan, 2002. (Simple Truth #25)

# Acknowledgments

*FROM KEN AND RANDY*

We both want to acknowledge right away the incredible partner Renee Broadwell has been during the writing of this book. She is not only creative and fun but her editorial skills are unmatched. This book would never have become a reality without Renee's help. We also want to thank our friends at Berrett-Koehler Publishers: Steve Piersanti, Jeevan Sivasubramaniam, David Marshall, and the rest of the BK team. You never disappoint us as our favorite publisher.

Throughout the book we refer to a number of Ken's coauthors and other leading experts in the fields of servant leadership and trust. They have taught us so much and we want to thank them for their contributions to our knowledge on these topics.

Thanks also to Danielle Goodman, Sarah Jane Hope, and Mike McNair, BK's chosen reviewers for this project, as well as several Ken Blanchard Companies colleagues and friends who offered their feedback on our manuscript. You all played key roles in improving the book, and we appreciate your help.

We are both thankful for Jesus, the greatest Servant Leader who ever lived.

## FROM KEN

I'm so grateful for my wife, Margie, and her continual support for almost sixty years. She's the best cheerleader in the world and a great leader in her own right. I'm also very thankful for our son, Scott, and daughter-in-law, Madeleine, our daughter, Debbie, and Margie's brother, Tom McKee, for their leadership of The Ken Blanchard Companies. And I want to express my appreciation for a few special colleagues: Anna Espino, Martha Lawrence, Richard Andrews, Vicki Stanford, David Witt, Michael Bowles, and Cheryl Horton.

## FROM RANDY

I'd like to acknowledge Ken and Margie Blanchard, the entire Blanchard family, and the founding associates of The Ken Blanchard Companies for the privilege of being part of this remarkable organization for more than twenty-five years; Pat and Drea Zigarmi for their enduring support, wisdom, and mentorship; Barbara Hart for teaching me "people are messy" and showing me servant leadership in action; Barbara Flowers for taking a chance on me in 1988; Keith Potter and John Tastad for letting a young buck take on leadership responsibilities beyond his years; Amanda Hines, Lindsay Ray, Jackie Glaser, Kelly Basham, Tracey Williams, Courtney Harrison, Kristy Curtin, Wendy Ruhm, and Patty Torres for being co-servant leaders of client services for many years and holding me accountable to walk my talk; and my colleagues in professional services who evangelize these simple truths around the world. Finally, thank you to my wife, Kim, and our sons, Michael and Matthew, for their lasting love and support.

# Index

goals
  BHAGs (big, hairy, audacious goals), 89
  good performance begins with clear, 16–17
  model behaviors that serve people, 67
  praising progress toward, 20–21
  seagull management of, 19
  SMART, 17
Golden Rule, 39
Goldsmith, Marshall, 5
good results. *See* organizational success
*Good to Great* (Collins), 47
Greenleaf, Robert K., 72

Hemingway, Ernest, 81
hierarchical pyramid
  the traditional, 13
  turning it upside down, 12–13
high-control leaders, 115
honesty, 101
humility, 47, 83

integrity (*integritas* or *integer*), 99, 101
invitation to follow, 59

Johnson, Spencer, 23, 25

keeping promises, 103
kindness, 89
Lao-tzu, 67
Lawrence, Martha, 77
*Leadership and the One Minute Manager* (Blanchard et al.), 29

leadership styles
  Coaching, 29
  command-and-control, 59
  Delegating, 29
  Directive, 29
  flexible, 29
  seagull management, 19
  Supportive, 29
  *See also* servant leadership
leaders/managers
  authenticity of trusted, 91
  either/or approach to leadership by, 29
  facilitating employees to care for customers, 35
  facilitating successful change, 61
  high-control, 115
  self-serving, 63, 69
  SLII® (situational approach to effective leadership), 29
  vulnerability of, 75, 83
  *See also* people; servant leaders; trusted leaders
*Leading at a Higher Level* (Blanchard), 61, 79
*Lead with LUV* (Blanchard and Barrett), 83
Lincoln, Abraham, 87
listening skills, 111
love
  1 Corinthians 13:4–7, 55
  servant leadership as action of, 55
managers. *See* leaders/managers
Miller, Mark, 69
mistake ownership, 109

money/compensation, 65
monkeys (problems), 51
motivation
    common sense common
        practice for, 43
    compensation and, 65
    good results tied to, 65
    identifying your leadership,
        79
    values drive our, 109

*New One Minute Manager, The,* 23
Nordstrom, 11

Olmstead, Cynthia, 77
Oncken, Bill, 51
*One Minute Manager, The*
    (Blanchard and Johnson), 23,
    25
*One Minute Manager Meets
    the Monkey, The* (Burrows,
    Oncken, and Blanchard), 51
"One Minute Re-Directs," 23
"One Minute Reprimands," 23
organizational change, 61
organizational success
    of customer care and increased
        profit, 35
    in facilitating change, 61
    as motivating factor, 65
    self-trust as first secret of
        personal and, 79
    trust as foundation of, 71–72
organizations
    compelling vision creates great,
        11
    creating culture of
        accountability in, 121

driving successful changes
    within, 61
motivation of getting good
    results for, 65
trust as foundation of
    successful, 71–72

Parisi-Carew, Eunice, 52
patience of ethical leaders, 99
Peale, Norman Vincent, 47, 99
people
    addressing their concerns over
        change, 61
    empowering your, 115, 121
    facilitating ability to care for
        customers, 35
    giving them a voice in change,
        119
    helping them to become
        autonomous, 37
    leadership is about serving
        your, 67
    motivating your, 43, 65
    recognition of your, 67, 91
    servant leaders invite them to
        follow, 59
    setting expectations with, 39
    *See also* leaders/managers
performance
    clear goals lead to good,
        16–17
    motivation of good results and,
        65
    praising progress, 20–21
    reprimanding vs. redirecting
        behavior and, 23
persistence of ethical leaders, 99
perspective of ethical leaders, 99

servant leaders (*continued*)
provide expectations, 39
serve their people, 67
side-by-side leadership
philosophy of, 53
take the first step in building
trust, 81
turn the traditional pyramid
upside down, 12–13
vulnerability of, 75, 83
*See also* common sense
common practice; leaders/
managers; trusted leaders
servant leadership
is about serving people, 67
the leadership aspect of, 9
as love in action, 55
as a matter of the heart, 95
the servant aspect of, 9
as a vehicle to building trust, 72
as a way of life, 136
*See also* leadership styles
*Servant Leadership in Action*
(Blanchard and Broadwell), 5–6
SERVE model, 69
show-and-tell game, 95
side-by-side leadership
philosophy, 53
Simple Truths
common sense common
practice to implement, 1–2
introduction to concept of, 1
Sinek, Simon, 5
SLII® (situational approach to
effective leadership), 29
SMART goals, 17
Southwest Airlines, 11, 83
Starbucks, 11

Stoner, Jesse, 13
success. *See* organizational success
Supportive leadership style, 29

Tate, Rick, 63
transparency, 105
trust
as construct between two
people, 87
control is the opposite of,
116–117
fear is the enemy of, 89
1 Corinthians 13:4–7 on love
and, 55
as foundation of successful
organization, 71–72
leaders have power because
they have, 41
relationships require leader
authenticity and, 91
restoring eroded, 125
self-trust, 79, 107
SERVE model on servant
leadership built on, 69
*See also* trust building
Trust Across America, 1
trust building
ABCD model of, 77, 81
apologizing for, 125, 127
demonstrating care and
building rapport, 93
by doing the right thing,
107
exhibiting vulnerability for,
75, 83
kindness contributes to, 89
leader authenticity for, 91
leadership begins with, 75

leaders making the first step in, 81
nurturing trust for, 87
as ongoing journey, 125
restoring eroded trust, 125
of self-trust, 79
*See also* restoring trust; trust
trusted leaders
admit their mistakes, 109
are good listeners, 111
authenticity of, 91
do the right thing, 107
empower people, 115
fairness of, 105
five Ps of ethical, 99
give people a voice in change, 119
inspiration of, 72
keep promises, 103
the power of, 41
restoring eroded trust, 125
truth telling and integrity of, 99, 101

*See also* leaders/managers; servant leaders
*Trust Works!* (Blanchard, Olmstead, and Lawrence), 77
truth telling, 101

values
control over our own, 117
drive our decisions, 107
identifying your, 79
servant leaders embody their, 69, 99
vision is driven by, 11, 37, 140
virtual workplaces, 115
vision
great organizations have compelling, 11
values drive the, 11, 37, 140
vulnerability of leaders, 75, 83

Warren, Rick, 66, 67
Wegmans, 11

# Services Available

# Join Us Online

## *KEN BLANCHARD*

Ken Blanchard Books website: https://www.kenblanchardbooks.com

Ken's biweekly blog: https:// www.HowWeLead.org

Facebook: https://www.facebook.com/KenBlanchard. Be part of Ken's inner circle.

LinkedIn: https://www.linkedin.com/in/KenBlanchard1/. Interact with Ken.

Twitter: @KenBlanchard

## *RANDY CONLEY*

Website: https://RandyConley.com

Blog: https://leadingwithtrust.com

LinkedIn: https://www.linkedin.com/in/randy-conley/

Twitter: @RandyConley

## THE KEN BLANCHARD COMPANIES

Website: https://www.kenblanchard.com

Blog: https://leaderchat.org

Facebook: https://www.facebook.com/TheKenBlanchard Companies

LinkedIn: https://www.linkedin.com/company/the-ken -blanchard-companies/

Twitter: @LeaderChat

Instagram: KenBlanchardCompanies

YouTube: Subscribe to the Blanchard channel at www.youtube.com/user/KenBlanchardCos

# About the Authors

## *KEN BLANCHARD*

One of the most influential leadership experts in the world, Ken Blanchard is coauthor of more than sixty-five books, including the iconic *The One Minute Manager*, with combined sales of over 23 million copies in forty-seven languages. In 2005, Ken was inducted into Amazon's Hall of Fame as one of the top twenty-five bestselling authors of all time.

Ken is cofounder with his wife, Margie, of The Ken Blanchard Companies, a globally recognized leadership training and consulting firm in San Diego, California. He also cofounded Lead Like Jesus, a worldwide organization committed to helping people become servant leaders.

Ken has received numerous honors for his contributions in the fields of management, leadership, and speaking, including the Golden Gavel Award from Toastmasters International and the Thought Leadership Award from Instructional Systems Association (ISA).

When he's not writing or speaking, Ken teaches students in the Master of Science in Executive Leadership (MSEL) program, cofounded by The Ken Blanchard Companies, at the University of San Diego.

Born in New Jersey and raised in New York, Ken received his master's degree from Colgate University and his bachelor's degree and doctorate from Cornell University.

## *RANDY CONLEY*

Randy Conley is vice president of global professional services and trust practice leader for The Ken Blanchard Companies. He is coauthor of Blanchard's Building Trust training program and works with organizations around the globe helping them build trust in the workplace. Trust Across America named Randy a top thought leader in trustworthy business behavior, and he is a founding member of the Alliance of Trustworthy Business Experts. Randy has also been named a Top 100 Leadership Speakers & Thinkers by Inc.com, and the American Management Association included him in their "Leaders to Watch in 2015" list.

Randy is the author of the award-winning *Leading with Trust* blog (leadingwithtrust.com). He is also a contributing author of *Leading at a Higher Level* with Ken Blanchard, *Trust, Inc.: Strategies for Building Your Company's Most Valuable Asset*, and *Trust, Inc.: 52 Weeks of Activities and Inspirations for Building Workplace Trust*. He holds a master of science degree in executive leadership from the University of San Diego.

Randy enjoys spending time with his family, cycling, and golfing. He's been married to Kim for thirty-three years, and they reside in San Diego, California.

You can follow Randy on Twitter @RandyConley.

# Berrett–Koehler
## Publishers

**Berrett-Koehler** is an independent publisher dedicated to an ambitious mission: *Connecting people and ideas to create a world that works for all.*

Our publications span many formats, including print, digital, audio, and video. We also offer online resources, training, and gatherings. And we will continue expanding our products and services to advance our mission.

We believe that the solutions to the world's problems will come from all of us, working at all levels: in our society, in our organizations, and in our own lives. Our publications and resources offer pathways to creating a more just, equitable, and sustainable society. They help people make their organizations more humane, democratic, diverse, and effective (and we don't think there's any contradiction there). And they guide people in creating positive change in their own lives and aligning their personal practices with their aspirations for a better world.

And we strive to practice what we preach through what we call "The BK Way." At the core of this approach is *stewardship,* a deep sense of responsibility to administer the company for the benefit of all of our stakeholder groups, including authors, customers, employees, investors, service providers, sales partners, and the communities and environment around us. Everything we do is built around stewardship and our other core values of *quality, partnership, inclusion,* and *sustainability.*

This is why Berrett-Koehler is the first book publishing company to be both a B Corporation (a rigorous certification) and a benefit corporation (a for-profit legal status), which together require us to adhere to the highest standards for corporate, social, and environmental performance. And it is why we have instituted many pioneering practices (which you can learn about at www.bkconnection.com), including the Berrett-Koehler Constitution, the Bill of Rights and Responsibilities for BK Authors, and our unique Author Days.

We are grateful to our readers, authors, and other friends who are supporting our mission. We ask you to share with us examples of how BK publications and resources are making a difference in your lives, organizations, and communities at www.bkconnection.com/impact.

Dear reader,

Thank you for picking up this book and welcome to the worldwide BK community! You're joining a special group of people who have come together to create positive change in their lives, organizations, and communities.

## What's BK all about?

Our mission is to connect people and ideas to create a world that works for all.

Why? Our communities, organizations, and lives get bogged down by old paradigms of self-interest, exclusion, hierarchy, and privilege. But we believe that can change. That's why we seek the leading experts on these challenges—and share their actionable ideas with you.

## A welcome gift

To help you get started, we'd like to offer you a **free copy** of one of our bestselling ebooks:

### www.bkconnection.com/welcome

When you claim your **free ebook**, you'll also be subscribed to our blog.

## Our freshest insights

Access the best new tools and ideas for leaders at all levels on our blog at ideas.bkconnection.com.

Sincerely,

Your friends at Berrett-Koehler